Grandma Was a Little Girl

Grandma Was a Little Girl

Kathy Smith Gemberling

Writers Club Press

San Jose New York Lincoln Shanghai

Grandma Was a Little Girl

Writers Club Press
an imprint of iUniverse, Inc.

For information address:
iUniverse, Inc.
5220 S. 16th St., Suite 200
Lincoln, NE 68512
www.iuniverse.com

ISBN: 0-595-22715-5

Printed in the United States of America

DEDICATION

To my granddaughters Ali and Madison, and others to come....

CONTENTS

LIST OF ILLUSTRATIONS

ACKNOWLEDGEMENT

With many thanks to my brother and sister-in-law, Barry and Jenny Smith. I couldn't have done it without you!

"My First Memory"

I was 2 years old. I lived on a farm with my father and mother and baby brother, Jimmy. I still slept in a baby crib. One night I stood up in my crib in the dark. I could see out a window and that night I saw a light. It was flashing. It was a long way off. I was terrified because I didn't know what it was. I had never seen a light like that. I cried and my parents came into my room. I showed them the light and they said it was a light for airplanes —to show them where the airport was. That is my first memory.

"THE SAFETY PIN"

I was in my parents' bedroom by myself, exploring. I found a safety pin lying on the dresser. I put it in my mouth and swallowed it. I don't know why. I just did it. Then I thought maybe I had done something bad, so I told my mother. She was very upset. She said to my dad, "What shall we do?" They talked about it for awhile. Then my mother said, "Was it open or closed?" I said, "closed." They said, "Oh, then you'll be alright." And I was.

"NEW MITTENS"

I had a pair of new mittens. I don't remember what they looked like, but I remember that I really liked them. I couldn't wait to go outside and wear my new mittens. I went outside. It was kind of cold, but not very, and everywhere I looked there was mud. I walked across the yard. Suddenly my feet were stuck in the mud and I couldn't move. I lost my balance. Helplessly, I fell forward and my new mittens went right into the mud. That was the end of my fun for the day.

"MY FIRST DRIVING EXPERIENCE"

I don't remember very much about this experience, but I'll tell you what I remember. Jimmy and I decided to get in the car by ourselves. I don't think we intended to really drive. I think we were going to pretend. Somehow we started the car. We didn't go very far. We ran into the farm scales. I don't remember our parents' reaction or punishment, probably because we were scared to death.

"THE WINDMILL"

I don't remember seeing Jimmy climb up the windmill. I think he was already up there when Mom saw him. Mom was too scared to climb up, and Dad had a broken arm (from a farm accident). Finally Dad decided he could go up and get him. The windmill was moving and I was scared to even move. Dad climbed up with his arm in a sling and brought Jimmy down. To this day I don't know how he did it.

"An Embarrassing Moment"

We were on our way home from Atlanta in the car. Jimmy kept saying, "I have to go potty, I have to go potty, I can't wait." Finally, Dad stopped the car and got out to help Jimmy. Just as he was going a car came behind us. I thought, "Oh boy. A car is coming. They're going to see us." Then, I couldn't believe it, the car pulled up behind us and stopped. It was some of our relatives on their way to visit us. I could have died.

"I Run Away"

One day I was thinking. I was thinking about our neighbors down the road. Their names were Ray and Ida Thompson. They owned the farm we lived on and they were really nice people. But the nicest thing about them was that they had pet rabbits on their back porch in cages and they would let you pet them. I decided to go visit them. So I got up off the porch step and walked down our long lane. Then I turned and started down the road. I was about 4 or 5 years old. When I got to their house I went up on the back porch and knocked at the door. They were really surprised to see me. I asked them if I could see their rabbits. Ida said "sure." Ray went back into the house. A few minutes later my Dad showed up. I thought he probably wanted to see the rabbits too. He didn't stay very long. He said I had to go home with him. When we got home we sat down on the back steps. Dad never did say very much. He didn't say very much this time either. He pulled me over his knee and spanked me several times. Then he sat me back down on the step and said, "If you ever do that again, I'll spank you again, but next time it will be with a board with a nail in it." I never did.

"The Horse Tank"

We didn't have TV when Grandma was a little girl, so we had a lot of time to sit around and think up things to do. It didn't always work out the way we thought it would. For instance, one day our friend, Larry, was at our house for the day. When you live out in the country on a farm, having a friend come over to play is pretty exciting. Anyway, it was hot and Larry and Jimmy and I were sitting on the back porch wondering what to do next. All of a sudden we looked at the horse tank out in the pasture. Somebody said, "We could go swimming!" Nobody hesitated. We all three raced toward the horse tank and jumped in—with our clothes on! Too late, we saw that the water was covered with a green slime. As so often was the case, no one had to punish us. Our foolhardiness had made us miserable enough.

"The Bull"

This is one of those adventures that I'll never forget. But I don't remember the "before" or "after"—just the exciting part. For some reason I ventured out into the pasture alone. Too late I saw there was a bull in the pasture. I had been warned about bulls, so I knew they could be mean. Sure enough, before I got very far, he saw me and started trotting toward me. It was kind of like a nightmare. My knees turned into jelly and I knew I couldn't make it back to the fence. The only other thing in the pasture was a big roll of barbed wire. Somehow I climbed up that roll of barbed wire and jumped right down inside it. To this day I don't remember how I got rescued from that adventure.

"THE POT-BELLIED STOVE"

In the middle of our living room sat a pot-bellied stove. The door had little windows in it so you could see the flames inside. One day Jimmy was riding his tricycle in the living room and accidentally ran into the door of the stove. The last I knew he still had a scarred fingernail from that one.

Another night Mom and Jimmy and I were home alone waiting for Dad to get home from town. Mom said to us, "I'm really worried. The stove just keeps getting hotter and hotter. It's getting so hot I'm afraid it's going to catch the house on fire. When Dad gets home he'll know what to do. Stay by me and if the house starts to burn, we'll have to get out." We stood by the door for what seemed like forever, watching for Dad and watching the stove. Finally, we saw the lights from Dad's car coming. And the house is still standing.

"SCARLET FEVER"

It was moving day. We were moving from the Thompson Farm to another farm on the other side of Atlanta. Grandma Miller, my mother's mom, was going to babysit Jimmy and me. We were at Grandma's when everyone started whispering and looking at me funny. I thought, "What is going on?" Pretty soon Mom came and said I had to go to bed. I thought, "This is silly," but I did. Then the doctor came! He took my temperature and said, "Yep, she's got Scarlet Fever." I told them that I felt just fine. I was sure that it was all a big mistake. I couldn't believe what the doctor was saying. "She is to stay in bed. No walking. When she has to go to the bathroom, carry her." I just couldn't believe it. I thought everyone was crazy. Well, they didn't give me any choice. I couldn't even have company. People kept coming to the bedroom window and smiling and waving to me. It was like a nightmare. Days went by and I felt fine. Then weeks! Finally, Mom and Grandma came and said that I could get up. But, they said, "we have to burn all your books, stuffed toys and paper dolls because they might make someone sick." I was just too young to understand. None of it made sense. Then, that wasn't all. I went to my "new" house (it was worse than the old one—it didn't even have paint on it) and found out that since I hadn't walked in so long that I couldn't walk anymore. I crawled around on the floor until my legs were strong enough to hold me again. What I didn't know was that many, many other children across the country were suffering from the same disease—practically an epidemic.

The doctor said I'd probably never be able to wear shoes with high heels, but he was wrong. Anyway, after I learned to walk again I just wanted to forget it ever happened and be a normal kid.

"THE FARM WITH THE UNPAINTED HOUSE"

Even though the next part of my childhood was spent on the rather run-down old farm, I didn't care. To me it was my world of adventure. We had no plumbing or electricity. That by itself was an adventure! Either stumbling way out to the outhouse in the night by flashlight or using the enamelware pot in one end of the kitchen on cold nights was commonplace. So was getting used to a sink that drained into a bucket below—the "slop bucket" that had to be emptied several times a day. Sometimes we forgot and had to clean up the mess. At night we did everything by lamplight. We took all this for granted.

We always had pets—dogs, cats, kittens, lambs fed by the bottle and, later on, a goat and horses. I remember that at first Jimmy and I had to sleep in the same bed. One night I woke up and felt something moving on my bed. I instinctively knew it *wasn't* Jimmy. I held my breath and stuck my hand out from under the blanket. It was warm and had fur! I was terrified. I yelled, and Mom came running with a light. It was a baby kitten. The next day I felt silly, but in the dark it was very scary.

"My Favorite Places"

As I said before, this farm was full of wonderful places for adventures. It had an old corn crib just right for playing house or just climbing up the slats. There was a barn with a hay mow. From up there I could see so far! There was an oil tank on high legs. If you could manage to crawl to the top of it, you could pretend it was a horse and you were riding it. The farm had a nice big pasture with little streams running through it after a good rain. I would sit by the streams and daydream that I was in another part of the world. I could be anywhere in my daydreams. There was a chicken house full of chickens. I didn't care for that place very much except when we got a load of new baby chicks so yellow and cute. I could pick one up and it was the softest little thing in the world. Then there was my favorite place—a little shed with just a lot of junk in it. Mom said if I cleaned it out I could use it for my very own playhouse. I cleaned it, swept it, unloaded the junk, and moved my dolls, doll furniture and anything I could beg or borrow out there and had my own little house. It was so wonderful and it was *mine*! There was never a dull moment on that farm.

"Our Pets"

I don't think I ever remember having a pet all my own. Our pets were a family affair. The first pet I remember was a dog named Puddy, named because he made puddles on the floor. Somehow Grandma and Grandpa Smith ended up with him and he lived to a good old age. Also I remember an all-white dog named Whitey, of course. Us Smith kids always came up with such original names! We always blamed Jim for the crazy names. Then later we had a Border Collie, a wonderful dog, with a white streak down his forehead. His name was "Lightning." Then there was "Stinky," the kitten who fell down the hole in the outhouse. Dad rescued him, I don't know how! There were others, a horse, goat, lambs, other dogs and lots of cats, but I don't remember the others' names.

"Going To School"

Along about this time I started to school. I didn't have an older brother or sister to tell me about school and in those days there were no nursery schools or kindergartens. You just one day went to first grade. My teacher's name was Mrs. Ferguson. She seemed very old but she was pretty nice. I think there were about 15 other children in my class. The first day Mrs. Ferguson asked each child to count as far as they could. I could count to 10 and so could most of the other kids. But one girl, Linda, counted to 100 perfectly. That night at home I told my mom and dad, "One girl counted all the way to the end of the numbers!"

One day I was sitting at my desk when I smelled a terrible smell. The boy behind me had thrown up. The most embarrassing thing that happened in first grade was when I accidentally called the teacher, "Mommy." The whole class heard me.

"Riding The School Bus"

The school bus was often the source of adventures. It was a trick to always be ready when the bus came, but not to have to stand at the end of the lane and wait for a long, long time. One day I was wearing one of my favorite dresses standing at the end of the lane waiting for the school bus. Just as the bus pulled up I somehow fell—into a mud puddle! I ended up missing the bus, changing clothes and being driven to school late by my mother. Another traumatic moment in the life of this child.

We lived the farthest out from town so we were the last to be picked up and the last to get home. The older kids on the bus took care of the younger ones. The bus driver picked two of the oldest kids to be "monitors." They kept order on the bus. We often played games and sang songs on the bus. Two of my favorite songs were "I'm Looking over a Four-Leaf Clover" and "Mockingbird Hill." One time our bus got stuck in the snow. We were about a half-mile from my friend Linda's house, so Linda and I walked to her house, leaving all the other kids stranded on the bus, including *my* brother. On the last day of school each year the bus driver would drive the bus route the opposite direction, so we were the first to get off instead of the last. One time I was sitting in the back all by myself (most of the kids had already gotten off), and the bus went by an old man standing by the side of the road with a shotgun. When I got home I found out that the man had shot himself. I was the last person to see him alive.

"All Tied Up"

One day in the middle of the summer we were at the neighbors'. It was hay baling time and we were helping the Pech family bale their hay. Jim and Larry (he was my age) and I were playing when we looked up and saw our moms in the car with the hay lunch heading for the field. I don't remember whether we didn't want to go or they just left us behind. Anyway, before I knew it Jim and Larry had dragged out a piece of old rope and were chasing me. Of course, they eventually caught me. Then, they proceeded to tie me to a tree. I didn't know whether to be furious or scared. I was probably a mixture of both. They just stood there and laughed at me. I didn't think our moms would ever get back. The boys saw them coming and quickly untied me before they could get in trouble. I was mad at Larry for a long time after that.

"My Diary"

I always kept a diary since I can remember. It had a lock on it and so I felt safe putting down all my secret thoughts. One day I did something really stupid. I took my diary to school with me. I don't know why, I just did. Well, you can already guess what happened. Larry, the same kid who tied me up to the tree, saw it and snatched it away from me. I don't actually remember what he did with it or how I got it back. It happened on the school bus and I remember my face turning beet red so I expect he read some of it to the kids on the bus. Larry and I are both "old" now, but he's lucky to have me as a friend after all these years, but we are still friends.

"A Wedding"

One year I received a bride doll from Santa Claus. She was very beautiful. She had real hair and I could dress and undress her. One summer day I decided to have a wedding on the front porch. I may have been inspired by the white flowers on the spirea bushes around the front of our house. I picked lots and lots of flowers off the bushes and laid them all the way across the yard, up the steps of the front porch and all around the porch floor. It was beautiful to me. It was probably the prettiest the front of that old unpainted house ever looked.

"Games"

Jimmy and I and our friends were always playing games. We played tag, hide–and–seek, dodgeball. I think our favorite was a racing game we played around the outside of the house. We would both start at the back step and go in opposite directions, all the way around the house. The first one back to the step was the winner. The exciting part was that you knew you would meet each other somewhere but never knew quite where. There was always the danger of running into each other! Proof that this was a favorite game was the "track" that went around the house, worn bare of grass from the pounding of feet.

"Measles and Chicken Pox"

Alas! Jimmy and I were both sick. I had the measles and Jimmy had the chicken pox. Poor mom with two sick kids. One thing happened that made this experience memorable. One day while we were all cooped up in the house we heard a sound of sirens, what sounded like a fire truck. Since we lived 5 miles from the nearest town this automatically meant excitement. Jimmy and I ran to the window and here came the fire engine—on our road! The next thing I knew Mom was yelling and pulling me back from the window. You see, the doctor had told her that a child's eyes were especially sensitive with the measles and not to let me out in the bright sunlight. I'm sure Mom thought I would be blind—but I wasn't. Where was the fire? I don't remember.

"Dennis Is Born"

One day about a year after we had moved into the unpainted house Mom and Dad packed up Jim and me and took us to Lincoln to stay with Uncle Connie and Aunt Marian and their three kids Ruth, Joe and Steve. Jimmy and I weren't quite sure how we felt about having a new baby, but it was exciting to stay with our cousins for a week. Jim and I were well cared for, fed delicious meals, and had fun playing with our cousins in the big city. Then finally Mom and Dad came to get us, and we all went home again— Mom, Dad, Jim and I and the new baby, Dennis Warren, because Dad's middle name was Warren. I was 6, old enough to help Mom take care of baby Dennis. I remember particularly helping Mom give him baths and when he got a little older playing with him with his toys.

"WINKY"

Just up the road from us was a real fancy farm with a house with white paint and lots of other buildings and lots of land round it. That's where Winky lived. His real name was Ralph, but everybody called him Winky. Winky was just the right age—one year older than Jimmy and one year younger than me. Just right for a playmate. Sometime during almost every day we went to Winky's or he came to our house. At his house we had a delicious time reading comic books—he had lots of them! At our house we played games and had many adventures. One day we decided to go camping. We took a can of baked beans from Mom's cupboard, a can opener and started off for the timber. We walked down to the timber, feeling good and sneaky, opened the can of beans, ate it and came home. That was our camping trip.

"The Race With The Rooster"

I told you that Jimmy and I loved adventures. If one didn't come up we made one happen. That's about how this one happened. We decided to climb up on Dad's John Deere tractor. Well, along came the rooster. He probably would have gone on up to the chicken house except Jimmy and I started calling to it. We managed to make it real mad. We thought it was real funny because the rooster couldn't get to us up there on the tractor. But, about that time Mom called us to supper. We were good and hungry and wouldn't have missed supper for anything. Jimmy said, "I bet we can outrun that rooster." I said, "OK". We both jumped off the tractor and tore for the house as fast as we could run. The rooster was right behind us. Jimmy made it. I didn't. He got me just as I got to the back step.

"Relatives"

Much of the excitement of my young life centered on family gatherings—aunts, uncles, cousins, and grandparents. My Grandpa and Grandma Smith (Dad's parents) lived just a couple of miles up the road. I enjoyed going there. There was always something going on and their farm had lots of neat places to play, too. Dad was one of six kids, so I had lots of Smith relatives! Usually, one of my cousins was there. There was Jeannie Foreaker, Dorothy and Bobby Smith, the Greenslate boys, Jeff, David and Roger, the McKay sisters, Mickey, Pat, Kit and Kelly, and Janet and Tommy Watt. Mickey was my age. She lived in Lincoln. Our favorite thing to do was play with paper dolls. But we did other things, too—playing in the barn, hay mow, picking grapes or flowers, playing in the coal shed and walking up and down their long lane. Grandma Smith had lots of hollyhocks, and Mickey and I made hollyhock dolls and floated them on water in galvanized steel buckets. Another favorite thing to do was walk up and down the lane looking for pretty rocks. We would bring the prettiest back to the house, wash them and have "rock stores." We pretended to buy and sell rocks.

Grandma Smith was a good cook and she always had something delicious to eat—cakes, pies, cookies, bread and jelly and more.

Another favorite thing I liked to do was sit and watch and listen to Grandma and my aunts and mom talking, drinking coffee and smoking cigarettes. They always laughed a lot. Mom didn't smoke or drink coffee, but she talked just as much as they did. Of course, later I learned that smoking is bad so I never did, but I still often think of my beloved aunts when I sit drinking coffee.

"Uncle Harold"

Dad had one brother, Uncle Harold. No one ever said much to me about Uncle Harold. A kid just listens and figures things out sometimes. Well, I figured out that Uncle Harold was quite a character. He had had three wives and never stayed in one place for very long. Most of the time no one actually knew where Uncle Harold was. But a couple of times a year we would look out the window and who would be walking up to the back door but Uncle Harold. He spent most of his time in the south—Texas and Arkansas—so he always had on a cowboy hat and cowboy boots. And he always brought presents! We kids were enthralled. We loved Uncle Harold.

"GRANDMA MILLER"

If there ever was an angel here on earth it was Grandma Miller. She lived in Atlanta. That in itself was wonderful. When I got older and became concerned about my social life, Grandma always let me stay in town with her so I could be with my friends. Grandma wasn't just good to me, she was that way with everybody. She spent her whole life doing for others. I wanted to be just like her. She always seemed "old" to me. One time I asked her, "Grandma, aren't you afraid of dying?" She said, "No, I have faith." Right then and there I decided that I was going to have faith in God, too. And I always have.

"ELECTRICITY"

As I said before, we didn't have electric lights in the country. Most people in town had electricity, but we didn't. After dark, everything was done by lamplight. Actually electricity was coming to rural America about this time and we all knew it. We could see poles lying alongside the roads and sometimes even see crews working their way out from town. We were a long way out from town so we were to be one of the last to be hooked up. Every day when Jim and I got home from school we raced to see who could be first into the house. You see, Mom and Dad had already purchased a floor lamp, and so we were ready. We even begged Mom not to tell us. "Just let us turn on the lamp and find out!" Well, the day that it happened Jim beat me to the lamp. I'll never forget that day.

"Surprise Birthday Party"

I was in the fourth grade and it was my birthday. I could hardly wait to get to school on this special day. It didn't take long for my happiness to fade. Up at the front of the room on a table were birthday presents. I had no idea who they were for. All I knew was that someone was having a birthday party and I wasn't invited—and on my birthday yet. I worried and stewed all day long. The only thing I could think of was that my best friend Peggy's birthday was a couple days off. Maybe the presents were for her. I couldn't believe that I wouldn't be invited to my best friend's party. Mom came to get me after school instead of me riding the school bus as usual. I was so sad and told her why. To my amazement she didn't even seem very sympathetic. We arrived home and I walked into the house. There were all my friends, including Peggy. It was actually a surprise party for both of us. She had just gotten there first. I nearly fainted. They had all stacked their coats behind the door. I remember just falling back on all the coats. You see, I had never heard of a surprise party before. Probably no one has ever been as surprised and as happy as I was.

"The Centennial"

I was about 10 or 11 years old. There was lots of excitement going on with all the adults. Atlanta was getting ready for its centennial. What was a centennial and why all the excitement? Then I found out—my hometown was going to be 100 years old. Wow! 100 years was a long time. First thing I noticed was that my dad began to look funny. He was growing whiskers. He sometimes had a little stubble on his chin. He used to love to "whisker" me—rub his chin on my face and tickle me. It made me giggle. But before long he had a beard. Lots of men in town were growing beards so they'd look like the men did 100 years ago. There was to be a contest to see who had the best beard.

But what was most exciting to me was that Grandma Miller was making long dresses for me and my mom and bonnets to match. We were to wear them in the centennial parade. My friends Laura Sue and Ruth Randolph were getting dresses made too, and our moms came up with the idea that the three of us would carry a banner in the parade with a big picture of a birthday cake on it. At the last minute someone must have been impressed because they asked us to lead the parade.

Something else I remember about the centennial was that someone built a playhouse that looked just like the Atlanta Community House and put it on a hayrack and pulled it for everyone to see in the parade. After the parade it was raffled off. I wished, probably even prayed, that my folks would win it. We almost did win it. In fact, our next door neighbors won it. They had three little girls, so I guess it was for the best. I remember getting to play in it a couple of times.

"PLAYING COVERED WAGON"

This goes along with the story about the centennial. One day Laura Sue and Ruth Randolph came over to play. We all three still had our centennial dresses. We took over one of Dad's old wagons and decided to "head west" like pioneers in our covered wagon. We had our "children" (dolls), all our doll clothes, dishes, etc., and our centennial dresses on. We really looked and felt like pioneers. Playing with Laura Sue and Ruth was always fun. We were always putting on plays and playing make-believe. One time we made mud pies and their mom, Holley, actually bought them from us! She was a good sport. She was also a good cook, so we probably actually got real cookies in return. I don't remember. I'll tell you more about my adventures with Laura Sue and Ruth Randolph in a later chapter.

"Girl Scout"

I was a Brownie Scout and later a Girl Scout. We met every week at the Community House. Most of my friends were Scouts too, so we always had fun. But we did do serious work, like earn badges and sell Girl Scout Cookies. Yes, even way back then we had Girl Scout Cookies, but in those days you could buy a box of cookies for fifty cents. We also went to camp at a place near Atlanta called Camp Gresham. It's still there but isn't a scout camp anymore. Two of my Girl Scout leaders that I remember were Mrs. Ford and Mrs. Ijams. They also belonged to my church and were both really nice.

"I Commit A Crime"

It happened in the Kroger store. I was shopping for groceries in Atlanta with my mom. She was busy picking out what she needed and I was ambling along just looking at things. Suddenly I spied a stack of numbers lying on a shelf. Somehow I knew they weren't for sale. They were the little numerals the employees slid along the metal plates under each shelf to tell you how much things cost. I must have been thinking about how much fun I could have with those numbers. I picked up a whole stack and put them in my pocket. As soon as we got to the car I pulled them out and proudly showed them to my mom. Her mouth dropped open and she told me I had just "stolen" them from the store. My mind was whirling! "Stolen!" Not me!" Oh, how embarrassed I was. Mom said I would have to go back into the store and take them and apologize to the manager. I hung my head. I guess she knew I was simply mortified. She said, "OK. I'll take them back and explain. But I don't want you to ever, ever do anything like that again!" I never have and I've never forgotten the terrible feeling I had at that moment.

"Bad Dreams"

Just like most kids I had my share of bad dreams or nightmares. Two I remember particularly. Once I dreamed that I was going to the bathroom. I woke up and I was—in the drawer of my dresser! I had gotten up and walked across the room in my sleep, opened the bottom drawer, sat down and…Oh my! Another time I had just finished reading a scary book about two kids who found skeletons in their attic. That night I again got up in my sleep, went to the top of the stairs and called to Mom. I thought I was telling her that I had to go to the bathroom. What actually came out of my mouth was, "I want some bones that aren't broken."

"Piano Lessons"

When I was 5 my mother and grandmother decided I should take piano lessons. I was so young I hardly remember much about those first lessons. I do remember my teacher was a Mrs. Lee. She seemed very old. Her house was dark and dreary. Mom walked with me the few blocks from Grandma's house the first time. Then she said, "You're going to have to walk here by yourself from now on, so you walk back to Grandma's after your lesson so we'll know that you know the way." I remember I was scared to death. I probably panicked, because I did get lost. I wandered around for awhile and finally saw the top of Grandma's big white house over the trees and figured out how to get there.

"MRS. MCINTYRE"

Mrs. McIntyre goes right along with the piano lesson story. Mrs. McIntyre was a lady in our church, a good friend of my grandma. I had been to Mrs. McIntyre's house several times with Grandma. Mrs. McIntyre lived between my piano teacher's house and Grandma's house. Now the important thing is that Mrs. McIntyre kept Hershey bars in her china cabinet. Every time I went there with Grandma, Mrs. M would give me a Hershey bar. They were so delicious. Even then I had a sweet tooth! Well, I got to stopping to visit Mrs. M on my way home from my piano lessons. I became quite a regular visitor! Then one day my best friend, Peggy, went to my piano lesson with me. As we left I started bragging to her that I knew this lady and if we stopped at her house we could both get a Hershey bar. Peggy thought this sounded great. So we went visiting. Well, Mrs. M greeted us at the door and told us how glad she was that we had come to visit. She invited us in and asked us to sit down. She asked after our families and we talked and talked…and talked. Nothing at all was said about whether we wanted a Hershey bar. I was getting uncomfortable. What would Peggy think? I didn't know what to do. Finally, I decided we might just as well give up. I couldn't understand what had come over Mrs. M. She never forgot! We politely said we'd better be leaving now and walked toward the door. Just as we walked out the door Mrs. M said softly, "Oh, by the way, would you girls like a Hershey bar?"

"The Tornado"

Mom was always scared of tornadoes. and probably because she was, I was, too. One time Dad saw one a long way away and grabbed the camera and took a picture of it. I was obsessed with that picture. I just kept going to the photo album and looking at it. One summer day I was at Grandma Miller's in Atlanta, because Mom had gone to a meeting in Bloomington with a bunch of ladies. My friend, Carol, came by on her roller skates and said why didn't we roller skate uptown to the dime store for some candy. I put on my skates and off we went. I remember that the floor in the dime store was an old wood one, creaky, but smooth for our skates. The Douthit's who ran the store allowed us to keep our skates on in the store. Carol and I were at the front of the store by the candy counter picking out our candy. But the sales clerk was nowhere to be seen. Finally we noticed that the door clear at the back of the store was standing open and the sales clerk was just outside it. She called to us, "Girls, come and see the tornado!" We quickly skated back to the back of the store, but that quickly it had gone back up in the clouds so that we just caught a glimpse of a tail swinging high overhead. We were still plenty excited, forgot the candy and headed for Grandma's. We couldn't wait to tell Grandma. Grandma was skeptical and didn't know whether to believe us or not. Before long Mom pulled up back from Bloomington. Carol and I ran outside excitedly yelling, "Guess what, there was a tornado!" Mom wearily climbed out of the car and said, "Yes, I know. I was in it." In our excitement we hadn't noticed until that moment the car—filthy with dirt, dents, rocks imbedded in it all over. Mom went on to tell us that she and her riders had seen the same funnel in the air that we did from the dime store, as they were driving home. They were driving right toward it. Not knowing what to do, someone suggested they stop at McLean and seek shelter. Mom told

50

them, "The only person I know in McLean is Alma VanNess." They said, "Fine, we'll go to her house." That's what they did. With the tornado bearing down on them they rushed into Alma's house, explaining as they looked for the entrance to the basement. Alma said, "You can't go down there, it's filthy!" But, Mom said, they went down anyway. Just as they got to the basement the tornado hit Alma's house. No one was injured, thank goodness, just the car sitting in front. Alma's house was the only house in town hit by the tornado!

Another year a deadly tornado hit near us. The strange thing about this one was that it followed a road called "Lazy Row" just as if it were a car. It even swung from side to side of the road just right so that it hit the houses on both sides of the road. No one around Atlanta will ever forget the "Lazy Row Tornado." I remember that after it was over we all climbed in the car after supper to go see the damage. I was so upset that Dad had to stop the car long enough for me to throw up my supper.

"DOING ERRANDS FOR GRANDMA"

I loved doing errands for Grandma. I would walk uptown all by myself, going by the Methodist Church, then the Prairie Farms Dairy, crossing the street and down to the post office. I learned at a pretty young age the combination to Grandma's post office box. It was so much fun to turn the dial this way and that and, as if by magic, the little door would swing open. The people in the post office and shops were always so nice to me. They would say to each other, "There goes Hazel Miller's granddaughter." Everyone in town knew Grandma and I never knew of anyone who didn't like her. I was so proud to be her granddaughter! I would leave the post office and often stop in at Goldie Williams' shop. She was a dressmaker, another friend of Grandma's. Sometimes Grandma would have me pick up something for her, but sometimes I just went in and looked at all the pretty "lady things." Then I would stop at the bakery. What a wonderful place! The smell was absolutely heavenly. They had all kinds of cookies—real big ones! And donuts, cream puffs, homemade bread. Grandma would send me after something from the bakery almost every time. I don't think, to this day, I've ever tasted a sugar cookie to match theirs.

Now to the best part of my errands for Grandma. Every time Grandma would ask me to go downtown for her, she would give me a list and go over everything I was to do. Then, just before I walked out her door she would say, "Oh, and here, Kathy, is a dime for something for you." That dime was so exciting. I would think about what I was going to get all the way downtown. Of course I had to go to the dime-store, the wonderful, wonderful dime-store. As far as I was concerned it was a child's dream come true. There were two rooms, one with everything from buttons to perfume to candy to dishes. The other room had toys in it—the kind Santa Claus brought. I usually never even thought of going into the toy room. To me it was unthinkable to even wish for anything any time except at Christmas, when Mom and Dad would go with me and help me look. I almost always spent my dime on candy. Even though it required quite a long time to decide which candy. Should I go for the quality candy and not get as much, or choose the cheap candy and get a lot? It was a big decision.

"Hay Lunches"

I think my love of baking came from making hay lunches. During hay-baling time all the farmers helped each other put up their hay. This required almost daily baking by all the women. If they weren't baling at your farm you were taking food to the neighbors'. Everyone—men, women and children—pitched in. The boys built their muscles grabbing bales in the fields and throwing them up on the hay wagon, or taking them off the wagon at the barn and fastening them to the long rope and pulley that hoisted them into the haymow. It was hard, hot work and after the hay was cut in the field it had to be baled as soon as possible so it didn't get rained on. The men worked from morning 'til night. So the women would usually fix a dinner and then a lunch in the middle of the afternoon. We made cookies or brownies or a sheet cake and lots of iced tea and lemonade and took it out to the fields. I loved helping bake and going out and serving the men and then sitting with everyone talking and joking and eating a brownie myself. To this day when I smell fresh mown hay, I get hungry.

"Christmas Eve At Aunt Dell's"

I was born into a close-knit family, as they say. For as long as I can remember anybody telling about, there are stories of family gatherings. The biggest tradition of my entire childhood was Christmas Eve at Aunt Dell's. Aunt Dell and her family lived in Normal, Illinois, about 30 miles from Atlanta. Aunt Dell was a widow, as was Grandma. Aunt Dell's husband was Grandma's brother. Our families got together other times of the year, such as Fourth of July, too, but nothing came close to Christmas Eve. There was never any doubt about where we would spend Christmas Eve. Along with the Christmas preparations at home, time had to be allotted for my brothers and I to learn our "Christmas pieces." These were poems or songs to be performed Christmas Eve at Aunt Dells'—in front of everyone, including SANTA CLAUS himself. Yes, every Christmas even Santa Claus came to Aunt Dell's during her party. What excitement! Nobody ever said what would happen if you didn't learn your piece—or forget it. That was just too horrible to even contemplate.

Christmas Eve finally came. Time to put our new clothes on and look our very best. Then a long ride to Normal. The only thing that made the trip bearable was the outdoor Christmas lights on a few farms along the way. Often the weather would turn bad, but did we ever stay home? Not that I remember. I remember one night in particular. It was so cold and sleet and snow were coming down. The roads were like glass. Our 1940 Plymouth crept along with a heater that barely prevented us from freezing to death. The ride seemed to take forever. The adults kept talking about whether to turn back or not. We finally made it. I don't remember coming home. Maybe we just stayed all night with Aunt Dell. I don't know.

Once we got to Aunt Dell's it was like a magical paradise. A beautiful Christmas tree, beautifully wrapped packages, candlelight, mouth-watering food waiting in the wings and all our cousins, dressed in their finest, as excited as we were. These cousins included the Hoose cousins (second cousins) and the Miller cousins (first cousins). The Hoose cousins were Nancy and Susan Hoose, Sharolynn and David Hoose, Heather and Gregory Hoose, and Melanie, Stanley, and Monty Cade. The Miller cousins were Ruth, Joe and Steve Miller, Joy, Jack, Byrdie and Libby Miller and Paul and Ron Miller. We didn't see each other very often, which added to the excitement. We would catch up on news of our cousins and try to keep busy so as not to get completely terrified of what we all knew was to come. We all knew that sometime Santa would show up, but nobody had any idea when. We were on pins and needles. Finally when we thought we could stand it not one minute longer there would come the sound of boots on the porch—and then the jingle of sleigh bells. The children would all hush and look at the door and at each other. The door would open and there he would be, with a pack slung over his back. The adults would fuss about offering him some punch to drink and a chair. Then he would say in turn to each of us, "Don't you have a piece to speak for Santa?" And each of us would stand up with knees of jelly and say our memorized piece. When each was done he would give us a candy cane and an orange. Then he was out the door and gone into the night. Pandemonium erupted. Our excitement could be contained no longer. There was giggling, laughing, yelling, wrestling. Then Aunt Dell would announce that the food was served in the dining room. Too excited to eat I still remember all that wonderful food— good cooks ran in the family. Days later I would wish for some of those mouth-watering dishes, but at the time I was too excited to take hardly a bite.

"Going To Lincoln On Saturday Night"

The thing to do on Saturday night was to go to Lincoln to shop. If Mom and Dad weren't going, Grandma and Grandpa Smith would usually take us kids. The most fun thing that I remember was sitting in the car with Grandma while Grandpa did his shopping, whatever that was—I don't remember. Grandma's true colors came out sitting in that car. We people-watched. Grandma would, from the privacy of the car, comment on all the people walking by. "Look at her, with her slip showing. She'd die if she knew." Or, "Look at that bald head. How can his wife stand him?" And so on. We would get to laughing so hard our sides hurt. I guess making fun of people as a child like that didn't hurt me. I would never do that today as an adult, especially to a child. But I didn't think any less of Grandma. That was just how Grandma was.

I remember going to Lincoln another Saturday night with Mom and Dad. We were walking past the dime-store. The dime-store in Lincoln was much larger and fancier than the one in Atlanta. They had display windows. Window shopping was wonderful. This particular night I spied a darling baby doll in the window. Mom and Dad came to see what I was looking at. I just couldn't tear myself away from that window and that doll. And it was only summer time. I never got a doll except for Christmas. I loved dolls—paper-dolls, girl dolls and baby dolls most of all. But I knew that there was no chance of having that doll because Christmas was too far off. The next thing I knew we were in the dime-store and a sales clerk was wrapping up that doll for me. Mom and Dad had bought the doll for me—for no reason at all. It wasn't even Christmas! That is one of my favorite memories.

"The Election Of President Truman"

As a child, the election of a president didn't mean much to me, but I got excited when my parents said they had invited friends over for the evening to listen to the election results on the radio. Not until the friends arrived did the adults discover that one couple was Democrat and the other Republican! What an unpleasant evening. I suppose the other couple left the happiest. My parents were the Republicans! And Mr. Truman, who became President Truman that night, was a Democrat.

"Easter Morning At Grandma's"

I remember Easter mornings with what I guess you could call reverence. I would stay all night with Grandma Miller. Then, first thing in the morning, we would get up and get dressed for sunrise service. We would head out the door very, very early for the short walk to the Methodist church a block away. But before we left, Grandma always made sure we had enough time to walk around her big white house to see if the Easter bunny had left anything. There were always bright colored real eggs in amongst the crocuses, jonquils, and little tufts of new grass. It was a special time just for Grandma and me.

"My Merry-Go-Round Dress And The Cloak Room"

Like any little girl I had my favorite clothes. Most of my clothes were made by Grandma, because there just wasn't enough money in our house to buy new clothes for, at that time, 3 kids. Even though my clothes were homemade, mostly I didn't mind. Grandma and Mom seemed to know what the other girls would be wearing and I was never out of style. They often let me help pick out patterns and fabric. Well, I had this favorite dress. I called it my merry-go-round dress, I think because it was plaid with lots of colors and had a skirt that flew out when I spun around. The skirt also had a ruffle around the bottom. I always felt simply wonderful when I wore my merry-go-round dress. One day, when I had on my merry-go-round dress at school, in the middle of class period a boy named Tom who sat behind me tapped me on the shoulder. Just as I turned around to see what he wanted the teacher looked over at us. All she saw was me turn around and talk to Tom. Without any questions she told me to go to the cloakroom. The cloakroom was a narrow long hall like a big closet off the main classroom with a doorway at either end. All along the wall were hooks for everyone to hang their coats, hats, etc. We were also expected to place any boots or other belongings neatly directly beneath our coat. Whenever a child was naughty this was the most common form of punishment—a sit in the cloakroom.

As long as I had been in school (I was in the fourth grade) I had never been naughty. I had never been punished. I knew I hadn't done anything wrong but was afraid to say anything. So I sat. In a little while it was time for a bathroom break. The teacher came to me and said that I might go with the other girls. As soon as we got to the "lavatory"—that's what they called the toilet—the other girls huddled around me asking me what I had done. I didn't have any problem telling them what Tom had done and that I hadn't done anything. I had just told my story when the teacher walked into the lavatory. She had been standing just outside the door and heard every word! She simply said, "Kathy, when we get back to the classroom, you may go to your seat." And that was the end of that. But I always remembered that I had on my merry-go-round dress that day. I hadn't thought anything bad could happen to me when I wore it.

"A Birthday Present For The Teacher"

In the fifth grade I had the same teacher that I had in the first grade, Mrs. Ferguson. We all respected Mrs. Ferguson and she was very strict. But Mrs. Ferguson was unusual in one way. Some days she was definitely in a great mood and other days she was definitely in a bad mood. It didn't take us kids very long to figure out which mood she was going to be in. As soon as she walked in the door we all knew. Why? If she didn't have makeup on she was in a bad mood. If she had makeup on she was in a good mood. It worked every time.

Well, one day Linda (the one who could count to 100 in the first grade, remember?) got an idea. She got us all together and announced that Mrs. Ferguson's birthday was coming up. We decided to each bring a dime to school, put them all together and buy Mrs. Ferguson a birthday present. There were 11 of us delegated to go downtown at lunch hour and buy something at the dime-store. The 11 of us were: Linda, Laura, Sue, Janet, Kay, Peggy, Carol, Judy, Donna, Sandy and me. This all sounded like a wonderful plan and we were all sure that from that day forward Mrs. Ferguson was going to love all of us.

The birthday came and the money was collected. The whole group of fifth grade girls trooped downtown to Douthit's. What we didn't anticipate was that we couldn't agree on what to get. We looked, argued, looked, argued, and looked some more. Finally, we agreed! We would buy lots of little presents instead of one big one. We finally picked everything out that we could agree on. Looking back I only remember one item—a bottle of cheap perfume. Heaven only knows what the rest of the stuff was. Well, that afternoon we proudly surprised Mrs. Ferguson with our gifts. She was polite. Somehow we all knew that somewhere along the line we hadn't used good judgment—we weren't sure just where. After that Mrs. Ferguson was her same self. We would have been better off with a polished apple.

"CHEERLEADER"

In seventh grade I was elected as one of the four cheerleaders for our class. This was no big deal to anyone except me. I loved basketball, had gone to many basketball games ever since I could remember. I was always fascinated by the cheerleaders, their cute outfits, the fun they seemed to be having, everything about them. I really wasn't very good, but I made it on the squad. Our colors were red and white and our nickname was the "Redwings." We had a big wooden "A" (for Atlanta) with wings on either side of it that we took to every game and proudly set it out in the middle of the playing floor.

The away games were especially fun because we got to ride the bus. There was always lots of excitement, cheering and singing on the way and even more on the way home, if we won! The thing to do after the game was to go to the local restaurant. It was called "The Palace Café." We often went there after school even when there wasn't a game. My friends and I usually had a Coke and potato chips or a candy bar. The Palace was the place to go. One favorite memory that I have of being a cheerleader is that after one game someone told me that Dr. Ijams, one of the town's two doctors, had been there and told someone, "Kathy's not very good, but she smiles a lot!" I liked Dr. Ijams—everybody did. And that's the story of my cheerleading.

"THE COUNTY FAIR"

The Logan County Fair was something that I looked forward to all summer. It was held in August. To this day when I think of the fair, all I have to do is close my eyes and I can picture every nook and cranny of the fairgrounds: the 4 –H buildings, the grandstand, food stands, trinket shops, animal pens, farm machinery tents, the Hoblit and Mountjoy Seed Corn tents (both companies from Atlanta), and, of course, the Midway with its games, sideshows and rides.

Our whole family would leave early in the morning and spend the whole day and evening. Mom would fix a lunch so we wouldn't have to spend our money on food. Sometimes we met friends there and spent the day with them, the women together, men together and kids off in two's or three's. We knew we could always find Grandpa and Grandma Smith in the grandstand watching the horse shows.

I remember one time in particular when I got to spend the whole day with my best friend, Peggy. We were in heaven! A whole day to ourselves—and, our parents had given each of us $1 to spend. What a mighty decision. Peggy and I walked all day going from stand to stand and ride to ride and food tent to food tent trying to decide how to spend our dollar. We finally agreed that we should spend our money on something we could take home. A ride would soon be over and food would be gone, too. The moment of decision was finally arrived at. We stopped at a trinket stand and bought ID bracelets, bright and shiny, and they even had our names engraved on them. We were so proud! We showed them to everyone. Now the truth shall be known. By the time we reached home both of us had green circles on our wrists. Neither of us ever admitted it to the other or to anyone else.

"MOVING TO THE BIG WHITE HOUSE"

One day the unthinkable happened. Mom and Dad sat us down and announced that we were moving to the beautiful big farm up the road, the one with the big white house. Winky's house! We couldn't believe it. Us, the Smiths living on that huge, beautiful farm. Winky's family was moving to town and Dad was being given the chance to farm the place. 600 acres and hundreds of head of cattle. Everyone was so excited. Mom and I sat in the kitchen of the little house with no paint and looked up the road and dreamed. Granted, the beautiful big white house had no plumbing, no bathroom, but the owners promised to put one in.

Finally the moving day arrived. This, after many hours of painting, papering, plumbing, and so on. We moved. My room was beautiful— pink flowered wallpaper and ruffled curtains. Downstairs was an entrance-way (for shedding work clothes), kitchen with built-in cabinets, dining room, living room, and Mom and Dad's bedroom. We lived on this wonderful farm for all my teenage years. Outside the house was a nice yard, a big orchard, and many, many barns and other outbuildings—17 as I remember. Picturing it today I would judge it was almost half a mile from the house to the farthest building, which was a huge barn. Beyond that about another quarter of a mile was Kickapoo Creek where we had lots more adventures, but I'll tell you about that later.

"CAPTURE THE FLAG"

Capture the Flag was probably our favorite outdoor game. We usually played it with the Brandt kids, but sometimes with others. First you divide into two teams. Each team had a white flag. The flag had to be white because this game was only played at night and you had to be able to spot the flag. One team would have its base as the yard on one side of the house; the other team had the yard on the other side of the house. Each team would hide its flag. The object of the game was to sneak across the other team's side, find the flag and bring it safely back to your territory. If you spotted someone from the other team on your side you would try to tag them before they could get safely home. If you tagged someone he was held prisoner at a designated "prison" somewhere on your side. Rescuing a teammate from the prison was also allowed, *if* you could find the prison and *if* you could both get back home without getting tagged again. This game was exciting and scary and that's why we loved to play it.

"The Cattle Bridge"

Our place was one of only a few farms that had a cattle bridge. This was a place near where the lane joins with the main road designed so that the cattle couldn't get out on the road. It was simply a bunch of boards laid over a ditch with every other board missing. The gaps were enough to intimidate the cattle, and it worked. At our place it also had many other functions. It was an obstacle course to ride your bike over, it was a tricky foot bridge to try to run over as fast as you could, it was nice to throw things down between the slats, just for the heck of it, and a kind of conversation piece if you had a friend over who'd never seen one.

"Kickapoo Creek"

We were also lucky that our farm bordered Kickapoo Creek. We weren't allowed down there by ourselves until we were much older, but that didn't matter because Dad would drop almost any job for an excuse to go down to the creek. He liked to fish. I could never understand why he liked to fish so well, because he seldom brought anything home. In fact, I don't think I remember ever seeing him catch a fish. He just sat up against a tree, laid down his pole, pulled his cap over his eyes and took a nap. It wasn't until years later that I learned that there was any other way to fish.

We also loved to go swimming in the creek. We would head out with Mom behind us yelling, "Now, be careful—there are big holes you can sink down in and that'll be the end of you!" We also had to wear our tennis shoes (without socks) because of all the sharp stuff on the bottom.

There was one place downstream that was known as "The Deep Hole" where we were never allowed to swim, only to fish. Supposedly the "granddaddy of them all" resided there. We never caught him.

"THE GARDEN"

Nobody wanted to help in the garden. But we sure all liked to eat what came out of it. If Mom announced that the garden needed weeding, I suddenly remembered I had homework or my room needed cleaning. If that didn't work, I would offer to tackle the whole house. The garden was full of interesting things: rotten tomatoes for throwing, peas and rhubarb that tasted great just sitting down right in the middle of the patch and having a snack, and crawly worms for torturing someone, *and snakes.* Dad said if he was out in the field on the tractor and Mom was in the garden and saw a snake, he could tell from clear out there.

"Wash Day"

We didn't have washers and dryers in those days. We had a wringer washer and two galvanized steel tubs in the basement. Monday was washday. Mom would gather up everything and haul it down. She'd fill the washer with hot soapy water and start the agitator. You always did the white things first, because you saved the water and, as each load went through, the water got murkier and murkier. After the clothes had "agitated" awhile each piece had to be fed into the wringer. It was like two rolling pins, one on top of the other. They turned and you fed the clothes between them and they came "squeezed out" on the other side into one of the tubs of rinse water. Next they would be wrung out again into a clean tub of water and finally once more and ready to dry. We'd dry all our clothes by hanging them outside on the clothesline. On rainy days there was a clothesline in the basement. But nothing smelled so good as clothes dried in the fresh air.

"Recipe For Fried Chicken"

Fried chicken has always been a favorite of almost everyone in the Midwest, me included. However, when Grandma was a little girl there was more to it than there is today.

First, Mom and I went out to the hen house. She would pick out one or two that seemed just right to her. (If we were having company it might mean picking out four or five.) First thing you had to do was catch them. That was tricky! Best thing was to corner them in the hen house by the fence. When she got the first one, she then had to wring its neck. I swear, it's true! That pretty much killed it. Then she picked up her butcher's knife and cut its head off. Then you just let it go. It would flop around for a few minutes and then lie still. This Mom had to do for each chicken, however many were needed. Next she would bring them in the kitchen and soak them in hot water. This made it easier to pluck the feathers. After a while it was time to pluck. Every feather had to be pulled out. Then she finally cut it open, pulled out the parts that you didn't eat and cut up the parts you did and set to frying it. As I said, I liked fried chicken as well as the next person. I just don't understand why Mom did.

"The New TV"

As I said before, when Grandma was growing up we didn't have TV. However, about the time I became a teenager some people were beginning to get TVs. My best friend Peggy's family got one and invited us over almost every Saturday night to watch. My favorite was "Hit Parade," a show which featured the top 10 songs of the week. No. 1 was saved until last and we practically held our breath waiting to see which song would be No. 1. Even though we did get to watch TV once in a while, you have to remember that there was no *color* TV, so it was still different than it is today. Other favorite shows of mine were all the cowboy shows: Roy Rogers & Dale Evans, Hopalong Cassidy, Gene Autry. There were a few others but I can hardly remember. I do remember that my favorite singer was Eddie Fisher and he had a fifteen-minute show every night around 5:00 or 6:00 o'clock and I never missed it if I didn't have to.

I didn't much like to watch TV at Grandma and Grandpa Smith's. Grandpa insisted on watching nothing but boxing. They advertised Carter's Little Liver Pills and Grandpa just sat and watched boxing and popped Carter's Little Liver Pills.

But what I wanted to tell you about was when we got our own TV. Dad surprised us. He just came bringing it home one day. I don't think Mom even knew. We were all simply amazed. We just couldn't believe that we, The Smiths, had our own TV! It was an exciting day, I tell you.

We still listened to the radio a lot when Grandma was little, too. I listened to "One Man's Family" and "My Little Margie" with Grandma Miller and we listened to "The Grand Ole Opry" at Grandma and Grandpa Smith's.

"The Escaped Convict"

I'll try to tell you this story the way I remember it. We got a call from the Brandts in the afternoon or early evening. They said that a convict had escaped from the prison at Lincoln. The police were looking for him and someone reported seeing a man in the cornfield by Brandts'. You see they lived close to Route 66 (what is now I-55) and it would have been logical for an escapee to follow the highway looking for a ride. The Brandt family was scared to death and Mom and Dad suggested they all come over to our house to spend the night. It was the middle of summer, plenty hot out and we didn't have air conditioning in those days. With so many people in the house the adults agreed the kids could all sleep on the floor in the living room for the night. Of course, all the windows and doors had to be left open to let some air in. I will never forget lying there on the living room floor all night looking up at the front screen door just waiting for that guy to appear. It gives me goose-bumps to this day just to think about it! And as things often go, I don't have any idea when and where they actually caught the convict. But *we* never saw him.

"The Night Dennis Scared Us All To Death"

While we're on scary stories, here's another one. As I said before, our wonderful new house was big enough for Jim, Dennis and I each to have our own rooms upstairs. When Barry was born he had a crib in Mom and Dad's room and later he and Dennis had twin beds in Dennis's room upstairs.

Anyway, this was when Dennis still had a room all to himself. One night we were all sound asleep in the middle of the night when Dennis let out the most bloodcurdling yell you ever heard. The gist of what he said was, "There's a man in my closet!" If you could have heard him you would not have had any doubt there was indeed a man in his closet. I think Dad took the steps about five at a time. Jim and I just lay in our beds, frozen with fear. The lights came on, there were a few seconds of silence, and then Dad yelled out, "It's OK, there's nobody here." You had to be there to know what a terrifying few minutes that was that night—another night I'll never forget. Years later Dennis told me that what he saw that night was a shirt hanging on the closet door.

"A New Baby"

When I was 13 the most amazing thing happened. My mom got pregnant. It was one of those things you never even thought about happening. Mom and Dad were real happy. Jim, Dennis and I were shocked. After thinking about it I decided it might be kind of neat. Anyway, the next Sunday morning after they told us kids, we were as always getting ready for church. Mom said, "Now don't you kids go telling people about the baby on the way yet. We're going to keep it a secret for awhile." I don't know what came over me but when I walked into the Atlanta Methodist Church that Sunday morning and looked up and saw the preacher, I just had to tell. I didn't think it would hurt to tell just *one* person. But telling the preacher was the wrong thing to do. He announced it to the whole church! I don't think I ever got the punishment I deserved for that one.

Anyway, after waiting for many months and weeks on December 9th, just before Christmas, we got our new baby. I was so sure it was going to be a girl. We were due for a girl. I was finally going to have a sister I'd always wanted. We kids stayed with Grandma Miller while Dad and Mom went to the hospital. We were there anyway, because Dad had gone to a basketball game. Mom had to wait for him to come to Grandma's after the game so he could take her to Lincoln to the hospital.

Anyway, next morning at 7:00 a.m. the phone rang. I lay awake listening as Grandma got out of bed to answer the phone. I heard her saying things like, "My, my, well, that's fine. They're doing all right then?" Nothing about, "Oh, we finally got another girl". Sure enough, she came back to bed and told me I had another brother. I couldn't believe it. How unfair!

I really don't remember this part, but Mom does. She said when Barry was a few days old she came in her bedroom and I was bending over the crib looking at Barry and said, "I'm *glad* he wasn't a girl!" And I've felt that way all the rest of my life. I wouldn't trade my three brothers for anything in the world.

One more thing about Barry—he smiled for the first time on Christmas morning. Grandma Miller was holding him. That I *do* remember.

"This Is The Church, This Is The Steeple; Open The Doors And See All The People"

This is one of the first rhymes I ever learned. Maybe the reason I remembered it was because I've always been a part of the church. I was baptized as a very little baby by a preacher named Rev. Geach with my parents bringing me to the altar of the Atlanta Methodist Church. Then as a toddler I remember Rev. Geach's fiery sermons, leaving me quaking under the pew. Later I remember going to Sunday school. Eva Ratliff was one of my teachers. Eva loved children but never had any of her own, so we were all loved as her own.

Then in junior high and high school I remember singing in the children's choir and in the adult choir, always next to my friend and fellow alto, Carol. Some of my favorite memories are of MYF, which stood for Methodist Youth Fellowship. We had MYF meetings on Sunday nights. The main thing about MYF was it was a chance to go to town and be with my friends. Don't tell anybody, but we used to go up in the sanctuary in the dark and play hide and seek and generally "run around." We crawled under the pews and hid in the Sunday school rooms. We never did any damage, just had fun. We also played hundreds of games of ping-pong.

Another wonderful game we played in the basement was called "Murder." The minister and youth leaders had to look the other way while we played because playing "Murder" in a church just didn't seem right. That didn't stop us. Here is how it's played: First you tear up a big piece of paper into small strips. All are left blank except one. On it is an "X". Whoever draws the X is the murderer. Then someone turns out the light.

Everyone just kind of walks around. Meanwhile the murderer finds a "victim" and taps him or her on the shoulder 3 times. The victim screams as loud as he can. The light is turned on. Everyone sits around in a circle. The victim stands in the middle of the circle. He gets to ask anyone if he is the murderer. He gets 3 guesses. If he doesn't guess he loses and the murderer wins. If he guesses right the victim wins. Then you distribute the pieces of paper and start over again. We never got tired of playing this game, but I'm sure the adults did.

"Church Camp"

Church camp was the only camp I went to for a whole week. I remember it was after Barry was born, because I missed him so much. My friend, Carol, went to camp too, so I had a friend when I got there. But of course you met lots of new friends. I remember sleeping in bunks, I remember putting on plays and programs for each other, I remember always being hungry! Also I remember worship services outside on a hill. I always felt so close to God up there. We studied the Bible and did crafts and other camp stuff, but my most memorable experience was also one of the scariest experiences of my life and one I'll never forget.

It happened at the swimming pool. We were all playing in the pool. I couldn't swim, but the kids convinced me to go to the deep end. They said they would hold on to me. For some reason the kids who had hold of me let go and it seemed like everyone had forgotten about me. I remember sinking to the bottom. I didn't have the first idea of what to do, so I just started walking along the bottom of the pool. Eventually I got to the shallow end and came up for air. Nobody had even missed me. Later when I thought that I could have drowned right in front of all the kids it scared me to death. But I don't think I panicked at the time, which may have saved my life. Anyway, to this day I'm still afraid of deep water and I still can't swim. I've gone fishing as an adult many, many times in deep water—but never without a life vest.

"THE EIGHTH GRADE MISTAKE"

I was in the eighth grade. Me and the kids in my class thought we were really "hot shots" because when you got to the eighth grade you had your classes in a room on the third floor of the school—with the high school. Anyway we also thought it was really neat to have a man for a teacher for the first time. His name was Dean Kampf and he was even nice looking. But we soon found out that men teachers didn't take any static, if you know what I mean. Anyway, it was near the end of our eighth grade year. It was a tradition for the eighth graders to go on a special class trip every year. We were going to the state capital for the day on the school bus. We had been looking forward to this for a whole year. Just before we were to go out to get on the bus, our teacher was called to the principal's office for something. He said, "I want you all to sit still in your seats and be quiet while I'm gone." And he left. He hadn't been gone but just a few minutes when two of the orneriest boys in the class got up and stood up on top of their desks. Then they started walking across the tops of all the other desks. People started to giggle and before you knew it pandemonium erupted. What we didn't know was that Mr. Kampf and the principal were listening to us from the office on the school intercom. Mr. Kampf came back with genuine sorrow in his eyes. He had to tell us that our class trip had been cancelled. Now that I look back I'm sure he was just as disappointed as we were. A sad day for the eighth graders at Atlanta Grade School!

"BLUE JEANS"

Until I was in high school the only people who wore blue jeans were boys, mostly farm boys. All at once girls starting wearing jeans to school. The girls who wore them were the really "in crowd." My dream was to have a pair of blue jeans and wear them to school—or anywhere. But Mom and Dad said," No." So I came up with another plan. I would sneak into Jim's room when he was gone and get a pair of his and at least see how I'd look in them. I could hardly wait. Finally the right moment came on a Saturday morning when everyone was out of the house. I opened a drawer and pulled out a pair. I stepped into them and pulled them up. What a surprise! They hardly came up to my hipbone. They were weird. I thought about it for awhile, sitting there on Jim's bed. I finally decided boys were made even more differently from girls than I had ever thought.

Maybe a year or two later I was finally allowed to wear jeans. As I remember, I could only wear them to ballgames or sleepovers and stuff like that.

"Going To The Prom"

Most people don't get to go to a prom until they're either a junior or senior in high school. But because our school was so small (about 125 kids) we got to go to the prom all four years if we wanted to. So I was probably not even 16 when I went to my first prom.

My boyfriend's name was Tom. He was tall, dark, and handsome—really! Mom took me to Landauer's department store in Lincoln to buy me a dress for the prom. I found it—the most beautiful prom dress in the world. It was yellow with yellow net over it. We even found beautiful little yellow butterflies to pin in my hair. I didn't think the night of the prom would ever get here. I would sit in my room and think of all the horrible things that might happen: I might get killed, Tom might get killed, the world might come to an end! But finally the day came. Even then I was thinking, "What if my hair turned out all wrong?" But just the opposite happened. I took the bobby pins out of my hair, brushed it and every hair fell perfectly into place. I had to admit that I had never looked prettier. Lots of people had told me that I was pretty, but they were my mom and dad, my grandma, my mom's best friend, but they didn't count. But that night I *was* pretty! I felt like Cinderella at the ball. The prom was in the school gym. It was decorated so beautifully that you could hardly even tell it was a plain old gym. Tom wasn't old enough to drive so we went with his older sister and her boyfriend. It was a night I'll never forget.

"Working In The Beans"

When I was about 13 Dad decided we kids should be helping out in the field. What needed to be done was cut the weeds out of the bean fields. Have you ever really looked at a bean field? They are very big. I think he told us he'd pay us 50 cents an hour. I was quite excited at first, thinking of what I was going to do with all that money. But as I climbed out of bed at 5:30 or 6:00 in the morning and trudged along the rows of wet beans, and often mud underfoot, the money hardly seemed worth it. Eventually as the sun shone overhead the beans and ground would dry out, but then we started getting hot, thirsty, hungry, tired and counting the minutes until Dad would say, "Let's quit for the day." The only time it was even slightly fun was when my friends Laura Sue and Ruth Randolph came to help us. At least I had somebody interesting to talk to and laugh with. They both had great senses of humor and made me forget my misery.

"MY FIRST REAL JOB"

After being miserable in the bean fields for a couple of summers, I was thrilled when the Randolph girls' grandmother asked us if we'd like to work with her in Waynesville, a very small town not far away. The only thing about this job was, I'd have to have a ride over and back since I wasn't old enough to drive and, besides, we only had one car in those days. Nobody had more than one car in those days. Also, it was a real strange job. Mrs. Adair, Laura and Ruth's grandmother, worked for a veterinarian named Dr. Starkey. Dr. Starkey had a deal with the University of Illinois in Urbana to experiment with a new way of delivering baby pigs. In those days lots of baby pigs got killed because when they were tiny the mothers would roll over on them. Dr. Starkey wanted to experiment with pregnant sows, delivering baby pigs by Caesarean section, then take the babies and put them in isolated cubicles, feed them until they were 6 months old, then turn them out in the pen.

Our job was to clean the cubicles. Have you ever smelled a pig close up? How about a cubicle a baby pig has been in for several days or weeks? It was pretty bad. Worse than weeding beans? I'm not sure. Anyway Ruth got the idea to bring her radio to work. That kind of took our mind off the work. But I haven't told you the worst. The cubicle would be crawling with maggots—still alive and wriggling and squirming! Again, Ruth managed to make the situation bearable. We danced to the radio as we worked, stomping on the live maggots as we danced. We called it the "Maggot Stomp." Only us kids could have thought that up and actually done it. Just to let you know, Dr. Starkey's experiment was a failure. Too many mother pigs died from Caesarean section.

"Blind Date"

Do you know what a blind date is? It's when you go out with a boy whom you don't know. Well, when I was 17 I had a blind date with a boy named Gary Gemberling. I had a friend from Atlanta named Joey Mountjoy and he was also a friend of Gary's. He called me and said, "I have a friend I think you'd like." He called Gary and told him the same thing. There was to be a sock hop at our school the next weekend. So the next day Gary called me and asked if he could take me to the sock hop. (That's where you dance in your socks.) I trusted Joey so I said, "Yes." I was so nervous. And Gary was *so* cute! Joey must have known what he was doing, because we went on more dates and before you knew it we were "going steady" (just dating each other, no one else)—and I was wearing his class ring.

"Dr. Drinkwater"

"Dr. Drinkwater" sounds like something I made up, doesn't it? Well, I didn't make it up, but someone did. It was the name of our senior class play. It was a musical. I never had a great voice, good but not great. Anyway, the music teacher chose me for one of the lead roles. I was so excited. I got to sing a duet with the leading man. The teacher also told me to lose ten pounds before opening night. I did! It was exciting and I played my part with all my heart. By this time I had met your Grandpa and we were falling in love. It was after the last performance of "Dr. Drinkwater" that he gave me his class ring. I always thought my duet with the leading man and the closing scene in which he kissed me long and hard convinced your Grandpa. He never admitted it!

"All Grown Up"

Gary and I went together for a long, long time—3 years. We had so much fun. We went to movies, out to supper, to parties, to ballgames—everywhere. Then he went away to college. A year later I went away to college. The same college! So we were together again. We went to more parties, dances, to Steak 'n Shake, Mother Hubbard's Cupboard, out for pizza, to ISU ballgames, and we studied together at the library.

By this time we had decided we were getting married. We wanted to wait until Gary was almost finished with college. We decided to get engaged on Christmas Eve 1961 and get married in September 1962. But first Gary had to ask my father's permission. This time, Gary was the nervous one! One night Gary came over to my house and sat down with Dad. He said," Mr. Smith, I'd like to marry your daughter." Dad just sat there a little bit. Then he said," My little girl has grown up." We decided that meant "Yes."

So now you know what Grandma was like as a little girl. Of, course, I couldn't begin to tell you every single thing. I don't remember everything. But now you know about some things that I did when I was naughty, how I was punished, what I liked to do, what scared me, and how I met Grandpa. Take good care of this book. Your children, my great-grandchildren, might want to read it some day.

ABOUT THE AUTHOR

The author lives in a log home in rural Atlanta, Illinois, her hometown, with her husband, Gary, her high school sweetheart. She enjoys spending time with her grandchildren.

0-595-22715-5

Printed in the United States
28717LVS00005B/214-261

9 780595 227150